Supersta[illegible]s

Teacher's [illegible]

Chris Hudson
With Margaret Cooling, Tracy Holmes and Gordon Raggett

Contents

RMEP
RELIGIOUS AND MORAL EDUCATION PRESS

Introduction

Who is your hero, and why? Pause for a moment and ask yourself that question. Did you name Martin Luther King for his speeches or his stand on non-violence? Was it Mother Teresa, for her compassion to the poor and the dying? No? Was it David Beckham, for that penalty against Argentina in World Cup 2002, or Jonny Wilkinson, for that final drop-kick against the Australians in 2003? (Sad, isn't it?)

Heroes or superstars are an enduring idea. The Viking sagas and Greek poets told stories of the great ones who did amazing things, usually a long time ago. The New Age writer Joseph Campbell declared that there is a common strand to stories about heroes in myth and legend. He said they tend to '… have a humble birth, some hidden flaws, but also an over-riding superhuman sense of personal dedication to some great goal or ideal'.

There is some truth in this – but many of our historical heroes are admired only because we don't know everything about them. Many British schoolboys were inspired by the story of Captain Scott's heroic failure in the race to reach the South Pole – without hearing arguments about how Scott's alleged ignorance of human nutrition and dislike of dog-sleds turned 'bad luck' into deadly disaster. That may change our view of the story. National heroes are often shown now by historians to have 'feet of clay', but this sometimes only makes them more endearing: they're not too different from us.

The 'superstars' in the stories covered by this *Superstars* Teacher's Book are all Christians. So why write about Christian heroes for young people? It's because we *all* have something to learn from them. These superstars don't fit the Campbell 'superman' definition; they're recognisably human, and they're not 'idealists' either. (A trade union leader once said that he never wanted to be called an idealist, because that meant people didn't expect him to achieve anything.) 'Idealism' goes back to the ancient Greek idea of 'spiritual reality' being more real than everyday physical reality, which isn't a Christian idea at all! Instead, these people either are or were simply trying to do the right thing by humanity and God, despite their failures and setbacks. They're like us, and they all made a difference.

But why bother telling these tales, when we live in a world where many adults and children in the West are now unfamiliar with basic Christian ideas? Here are some reasons.

First, whether one likes it or not, Christianity has been a powerful force in the world for over 1500 years, and continues to be the world religion with not only the most believers, but the greatest diversity of believers around the world. You will find them in almost every country and culture, because Christianity is not dependent on any one culture for its strength. Children from all faiths (and none) need to be aware of this multi-coloured world heritage to be properly educated, especially if they live in a country with a long tradition of Christian belief. Any understanding of British and Irish (let alone European) history has to take account of the influence (good and bad) of Christianity through the centuries.

Secondly, we need to consider the continuing impact of Christian thought and action in the world. Millions of people live and work with the idea that God is interested both in them and in how they live, and that God is best understood through the life and ministry of Jesus. This has an influence on how they spend their money, raise their children, on how they vote – and even on how they fight. In the global village, many of our neighbours are Christian, and we need to take note of it.

Thirdly, there is the continuing need of people to be in touch with the spiritual world. In the prosperous West, this becomes most apparent in times of national or personal disaster. At the point of trauma, there is a strong desire to make sense of things by reaching beyond the physical, to seek a greater security 'out there'. It's no coincidence that in the last century, the greatest growth point for British churches came during the trauma of World War 2. The stories in the *Superstars* books point towards a profound sense of security based not just on the material world, but on the spiritual as well. For these people, God was real and at work in their lives – let's learn from them.

Making the Most of the Superstars Books

The *Superstars* pupils' books may be used in a variety of ways: for example, just as storybooks or as an assembly resource – but they are chiefly designed for classroom use in RE, Citizenship/PHSE and/or Literacy. This teacher's book suggests some possible learning objectives and activities for RE, Citizenship/PSHE/Thinking Skills and Language, Literacy and Drama work for each story in the *Superstars* books *Warriors of World War 2, To the Rescue* and *It's Tough at the Top* (also published in a single volume as *Superstars Omnibus I*). Don't try to do all of the activities! You, the teacher, will need to select the appropriate focus to fit your school's schemes of work. To help you do this, the 'Curriculum Links' table on pages 4-5 lists key words and phrases relating to RE and Citizenship/PSHE syllabuses with Thinking Skills to show how each story might be used.

The Literacy levels are suitable for good readers from the age of 10+, who should be able to tackle the stories independently. Less-able and younger readers will need guided reading sessions with teacher support to get the most out of these resources. A glossary for each story is provided in this book.

The teaching suggestions include a wide range of tasks to be organised in a variety of ways in the classroom. For example, *Discuss* or *Brainstorm* could be an activity for pairs, small groups or the whole class, with teacher intervention as required. Instructions and questions preceded by *Task* are aimed at pupils, not teachers. Some Literacy activities reinforcing pupils' comprehension of the story could be used to support work in RE or Citizenship/PSHE. You will need to use your own professional judgement as to which are the best teaching suggestions for your class and scheme of work – but do make the most of the variety available. They will support both your differentiation in lesson planning (to allow for pupil ability), and your development of Thinking Skills in the subject.

Some teaching suggestions refer to the Bible. It should be noted that most Christians see nothing wrong in using the Bible to meet Literacy objectives, providing that the point is made that this book is very special for members of that faith community and should therefore be shown respect. Your pupils may benefit from a specific lesson that explains how the biblical book, chapter and verse system works (a useful reference skill in itself) and gives them a chance to try it out for themselves, hunting for specific passages on a given theme.

Artistic Licence

This book also gives you more background information about the stories. A lot of research went into writing them, but I have made obvious concessions for a young twenty-first century audience. Most of the speech patterns are modern, although I have tried to avoid obvious anachronisms in vocabulary. Where original written text is reproduced, I have sometimes inserted words that clarify the meaning of the passage to make comprehension easier. A great many of the conversations are based on original records, but obviously made some time after the event in question. Invented characters or events are also noted.

The subjects of the 'modern' stories have all had the opportunity to comment on their 'treatment', and I am grateful for their feedback. The subjects of the 'older' stories will no doubt give me their opinion one day. Any mistakes (especially the one in *Wings* that claimed Victoria Crosses are only awarded on a posthumous basis) are naturally, mine.

CH

Curriculum Links for RE and Citizenship/ PSHE/Thinking Skills

The *Superstars* stories may be used in a variety of ways to deliver aspects of RE, Citizenship / PSHE and Thinking Skills. This table is designed to help you tie in particular stories and activities with your own school schemes of work for these curriculum areas.

The **Possible Learning Objectives** (also listed at the beginning of the notes for each story) indicate some important ideas and issues that may be explored through the stories and the teaching suggestions provided below.

All the stories and corresponding RE teaching suggestions contain material that would enable you to cover aspects of the following RE themes:
- The difference that faith makes
- Moral values and attitudes
- Personal responsibility
- Beliefs

The **RE Key Words** indicate further themes common to most RE syllabuses covered in the stories and teaching suggestions.

All the Citizenship / PSHE / Thinking Skills activity sections (when used with the stories) give pupils the opportunity to:
- Express opinions
- Develop self-worth
- Research and discuss issues
- Reflect on spiritual and moral issues
- Consider moral choices and social dilemmas
- Find information and / or advice

The **Citizenship/PSHE/Thinking Skills Key Words** indicate in more detail the topics that could be addressed.

	Story	Possible Learning Objectives The stories and the teaching suggestions in this book give pupils the opportunity to consider:	RE Key Words	Citizenship/ PSHE/Thinking Skills Key Words
Warriors of World War 2	**The Secret War** Charles Fraser-Smith	• The idea of using one's mind and talents to serve God • Christian attitudes to war • How skills and abilities may be developed and used • The value of problem-solving skills	Ultimate questions Making sense of life	Problem-solving Conflict resolution and Peace
	Wings Cyril Barton VC	• What it means to be strong • Self-sacrifice and related Christian beliefs about the death of Jesus • Different attitudes to death • Whether war is ever justifiable	Ultimate questions Making sense of life Compassion for others Death and bereavement	Conflict resolution and Peace Responsibilities Europe
	Hospitality Frank Foley	• How we should treat vulnerable people, such as refugees • Christian beliefs about taking action to protect and care for others • Images from the Bible of God as protector	Persecution Justice Compassion for others Anger Authority	Racism and Prejudice Helping others Keeping safe Diversity Human rights

	Story	Possible Learning Objectives The stories and the teaching suggestions in this book give pupils the opportunity to consider:	RE Key Words	Citizenship/ PSHE/Thinking Skills Key Words
To the Rescue	**Mission** Samuel Papenekis	• How Christianity can flourish in different cultures throughout the world • Christian teachings that may have motivated the Indians who undertook the rescue mission • The importance of worship to Christians • Whether it is right to try to persuade others to change their attitudes or religious beliefs	World Church Compassion for others My community Death and bereavement	Diversity Community Keeping safe Helping others
	The Darkness Corrie ten Boom	• Responses to suffering, including a Christian response • Light and darkness as symbols of good and evil • Aspects of human rights, including how peoplewith learning difficulties should be treated	Persecution Justice Reconciliation Compassion for others My community	Human rights Diversity Discrimination Helping others
	Hunter The A Rocha Trust	• Different attitudes to animals and the environment • Social issues relating to guns	World Church Responses to the environment	Moving on Media Rules and laws Laws protecting animals The Environment
It's Tough at the Top	**Riot!** Toyohiko Kagawa	• What is involved in being a peacemaker • How religious faith or personal beliefs influence important decisions people make about their lifestyle and actions • Whether or not protests against injustice should be non-violent • What makes a good leader • Protection of workers' rights	Justice Reconciliation Compassion for others Anger My community Authority World Church	Conflict resolution and Peace Democracy Human rights
	Surrender Chris Keeble	• Difficulties leaders may face, such as having to make tough decisions • Prayer as a response to difficult situations • Negotiation as a way of resolving disputes	Prayer Reconciliation Obedience Authority	Conflict resolution and Peace Responsibilities Problem-solving
	Peacemaker Pocohontas	• Different styles of leadership • What Jesus said about being a leader • What it means to be a Christian • Skills required to be a peacemaker	Reconciliation Authority	Conflict resolution and Peace Responsibilities

Warriors of World War 2

The Secret War

Charles Fraser-Smith

*Warriors of World War 2, pages 3-12 * Omnibus I, pages 7-16*

Possible Learning Objectives

This story and the teaching suggestions below give pupils the opportunity to consider:

- the idea of using one's mind and talents to serve God
- Christian attitudes to war
- how skills and abilities may be developed and used
- the value of problem-solving skills

The story also provides examples of how Christians pray and read the Bible for guidance in their daily lives.

The photocopiable *The Secret War* activity/assessment sheet (see page 27) focuses on pupils' own skills and how these could be improved.

The teaching suggestions for this story complement the activities suggested for:

- *Hospitality*, the story about Frank Foley; see pages 10-12 of this book;
- *The Apple*, the play about Isaac Newton in the Superstars book *Mind Stretchers*; see *Superstars Teacher's Book II* (pages 24-26).

Background to the Story

Charles Fraser-Smith was the real-life original for Ian Fleming's 'Q', the inventor of amazing fantasy gadgets for James Bond. Charles didn't think much of the 007 stories and films because of the way they glorified fighting. He always saw war as 'a depraved business', and he was doing his best to end it by working for the side that he thought best served God. (He wasn't particularly happy about the sex scenes in the books and films, either!) Fraser-Smith was an extremely practical multi-lingual missionary with fascinating experiences of running farms and orphanages in the Arab world – not bad, for a boy who left school with hardly any qualifications! His life shows that there's more to intelligence than academic brilliance, and suggests that we may all have hidden talents still waiting to be discovered.

Teaching Suggestions

Introducing the Story

It would be worthwhile to introduce a class teaching session by showing a short (age-appropriate) clip of a 'Q' scene from a James Bond film. Explain that you will be looking at the life of the real 'Q', who was a Christian who believed in using his mind to serve God.

RE Activities

1 *Discuss* how Charles Fraser-Smith believed he could be part of a 'secret war' and still be a Christian. *Ask:* 'What questions do you think he asked himself about this? Do you think there were any "jobs" that he would have refused to work on?'

2 *Ask:* 'Do you think your mind is important?' *Discuss* what it means to be 'clever' or intelligent. When could it be a good thing? When could it be a bad thing?

Task: Find and copy out some dictionary definitions of 'wisdom'. Then read Proverbs 3:1-8, 13-24, 4:1-27. What do you think these Bible passages are saying about how we think? What are they saying about learning?

3 *Read* Jesus' parable about the wise and foolish investors (Matthew 25:14-30). (The sums of money involved are often translated in English as 'talents', which can lead into a discussion of using one's personal talents to the full.) *Explain* that this is a useful picture for discussing the way people use (or misuse) the skills and abilities they may have.

Task: What do you think your talents are? (Think as widely as possible.) List all the things that you are good at. Discuss these with two other people – do they have anything to add? Are you developing these talents as much as possible? What good things could they be used for? How would you like to see them being used in future? How might a Christian think those talents could be used to serve God?

Citizenship/PSHE/ Thinking Skills

1 *Use* a variety of graphics to illustrate the worth of techniques such as flow charts and 'mind-mapping' to help someone think their way into and through a problem. For more information, see the work done on 'mind-mapping' by Tony and Barry Buzan (see Bibliography, page 32). *Then consider* a school problem (litter?), and use the techniques to brainstorm ideas, listing all the possible factors that affect the problem, and possible solutions. Edward De Bono's 'lateral thinking' books also provide lots of ideas for this (see Bibliography, page 32). Slogans for classroom display could include CAF (Consider All Factors) and 'Think Now, Judge Later'.

2 *Task:* Create a classroom display of child-friendly problem-solving puzzles and publications such as *Aquila* and *The Anti-Colouring Book* (see Bibliography, page 32).

3 *Discuss* the rights and wrongs of keeping secrets, including the idea that there could be such a thing as a 'bad' secret, if it is being forced on you by someone else.

Language, Literacy and Drama Work

1 *Task:* Use the information provided to create an illustrated potted biography of Charles Fraser-Smith entitled 'The Man who was Q'.

2 *Explain* that the original James Bond novels were written in a time when the UK and USA were close to being at war with Russia (or as it was then, the USSR). The world has changed since then, and the later James Bond films reflect this, relying on more clever gadgets than the books did. *Discuss* the attractions of the fantasy world of James Bond and similar 'spies'– why do so many people like the idea of being a secret agent? *Use this* as a stimulus for creative writing, e.g. 'My life as a secret agent'.

3 *Ask:* 'What does a secret agent look like?' *Discuss* the stereotypical images – and compare them with the real thing.

Task: Why is secrecy considered to be glamorous? Why wouldn't glamour work very well for a real agent? Write a recruitment advertisement for a job in the secret service – what sorts of skills and talents do you think they would *really* be looking for?

4 *Discuss* the elements that go into making a typical scene from a James Bond film, obviously avoiding sex scenes and gratuitous violence. *Task:* Script a parody of a scene from a James Bond film – perhaps in this version, everything goes wrong for him! [Award extra marks for anyone who uses the phrase 'So, Mr Bond – we meet again…'.]

5 *Study* the use and effect of 'asides' in the story to show how Charles' mind was working. *Task:* Use this technique to describe five minutes in a playground setting, for one of your friends.

6 *Task:* Create a 'Choose your own adventure' book where the reader has to make a series of choices to reach one of a range of possible endings. The book's structure will need to be modelled first as a kind of decision tree.

Glossary

Official Secrets Act – People working for the UK government have to promise not to tell anyone about their work or about anything they know because of their job. They have to sign a special document to show they understand this. It is *very* important!
Dealers – People who buy and sell.
Forged – Copied, but not real. It is against the law to forge banknotes or coins.

Wings
Cyril Barton

*Warriors of World War 2, pages 13-22 * Omnibus I, pages 17-26*

Possible Learning Objectives

This story and the teaching suggestions below give pupils the opportunity to consider:
- what it means to be strong
- self-sacrifice and related Christian beliefs about the death of Jesus
- different attitudes to death
- whether war is ever justifiable

The photocopiable *Wings* activity/assessment sheet (see page 27) focuses on Cyril Barton's attitudes to life (and death) and asks pupils to design a medal for someone they regard as brave.

Background to the Story

The Allied bombing campaign of World War 2 is still controversial. The Allied commanders believed that the best way to destroy German morale was to 'carpet-bomb' major cities in Germany. Hindsight tells us that this didn't work – but hindsight is easy 70 years later, when you are not fighting a war. There certainly *was* an understandable British desire to revenge the punishment that the German Luftwaffe had dealt out to cities like Coventry. However, people can sometimes become *even more* determined when they suffer something like an attack on their country or city. Historians talk about 'the spirit of the Blitz' in wartime Britain, but something similar was happening in German cities too.

Despite this, we can easily forget that for many, the war against the Nazis was (and still is) a clear case of Good versus Evil – and this was *before* people had heard about the death camps. There was plenty of evidence to show that Hitler's New Order had very different standards of morality to Christianity, and many (including Winston Churchill) believed that the war had to be fought on the behalf of Christian civilisation. That's why people like Cyril Barton were prepared to fight. His Christian faith was individual and intelligent, sustaining him in what he was doing. It's probably no coincidence that church attendance in Britain reached its highest level in the twentieth century during the hardship and struggle of World War 2.

Freddie's 'letter' is a piece of fiction based on first-hand descriptions of what happened on the night of 30-31 March 1944.

Teaching Suggestions

Introducing the Story

When using this story with children, you may need first to recount some basic details of World War 2, if they haven't already covered this period in their history lessons. Some video footage of Allied bombing raids would be especially useful. (Clips from the film *Memphis Bell* would be better than nothing!)

Before the story is read, ask: 'What do you think it's like to fight in a real war? Don't be fooled by the films – it's a *lot* more scary than you'd think, and it's sometimes very hard to work out what's the *right* thing to do. Can you kill people and still be a good person? See what *you* think about the hero of this story.'

RE Activities

1. *Ask:* 'What do we know about Cyril, from the story? What do we know about his attitudes to what he was doing? In your opinion, how did those attitudes affect the way he died?' (See also *Wings* activity/assessment sheet, page 27.)

2. *Discuss* what it means for someone to be strong. In his letter, Freddie makes the comment, 'His faith in God is strong.' *Ask:* 'What does this mean? How did this affect what Cyril did? After his death, Cyril was awarded the Victoria Cross, which has the words "For Valour" inscribed upon it. What is valour? If you could award someone a medal, who would it be, and what would it be for?' (See also *Wings* activity/assessment sheet, page 27.)

3. *Ask:* 'What is self-sacrifice? Can you think of examples of people sacrificing themselves on behalf of others? Christians believe that when Jesus died, he was sacrificing himself on behalf of his friends, and the whole human race. Does self-sacrifice always have to involve death? Can you think of examples where people have devoted their whole lives on behalf of others?'

4. *Brainstorm*: 'What different images and symbols do we associate with death? What do they say about our attitude to it? What do you think Cyril's attitude was? (Why do you think Christians use the Cross as their symbol, when it is a reminder of death?)'

5 *Read* Ecclesiastes 3:1-8. *Ask:* 'Do you think this is simply describing what happens, or is it telling people how to live? Why?'

Citizenship/PSHE/ Thinking Skills

1 *Hot-seat* 'Cyril' and another member of the crew, asking them questions about their roles in the story.

2 *Set up* a 'Conscience Alley' exercise to explore the question 'Is war ever right?' Two lines of pupils should sit facing each other on chairs. Each child has to think of one reason why Cyril should or shouldn't be a bomber pilot, with the *Yes, he shoulds* on one side and the *No, he shouldn'ts* on the other. One child role-plays Cyril, who walks along the line, asking each child what they think – and then decides whether or not to be a bomber pilot. Which were the arguments that swayed 'Cyril' most?

Language, Literacy and Drama Work

1 *Task:* Write a reply from Freddie's mum to his letter.

2 *Read and display* the layout of George Herbert's poem 'Easter-wings' (see Bibliography, page 32). *Task:* Write an acrostic poem on one of the themes covered in this unit, but in the shape of something appropriate – such as a pair of wings, or an aircraft.

Glossary

Wings – The RAF badge includes a pair of wings.
Careless talk costs lives – A slogan that warned against revealing important secrets to enemy spies by mistake.
Censor – Here, to delete important information from a text so that it doesn't reveal secrets.
Searchlights – Giant lights designed to spot enemy aircraft at night, so they can be shot at.
Barrage balloons – Giant balloons trailing long metal cables designed to make a plane crash if it hits them.
Fuselage – Main body of a plane, between the nose and the tail.
Navigator – Here, aircraft crew member in charge of making sure that they don't get lost.
Dormitory – Large shared bedroom with lots of beds.

Hospitality

Frank Foley

*Warriors of World War 2, pages 23-31 * Omnibus I, pages 27-35*

Possible Learning Objectives

This story and the teaching suggestions below give pupils the opportunity to consider:

- how we should treat vulnerable people, such as refugees
- Christian beliefs about taking action to protect and care for others
- images from the Bible of God as protector

The photocopiable *Hospitality* activity/assessment sheet (see page 28) focuses on what helps people to feel safe.

The teaching suggestions for this story complement the activities suggested for:

- *The Secret War*, the story about Charles Fraser-Smith; see pages 6-8;
- *The Darkness*, the story about Corrie ten Boom; see pages 15-17.

Background to the Story

The story of Oscar Schindler became widely known with the publication of Thomas Keneally's book *Schindler's Ark*, which was then made into the film *Schindler's List*. Perhaps something similar will happen one day for Frank Foley. He saved the lives of at least ten thousand Jews (and other potential victims of the Nazis) by stretching every rule possible, enabling emigration from Nazi Germany prior to the outbreak of World War 2. Not only was he a humane bureaucrat – he was actually the Head of the British Secret Service in Germany, living a very dangerous double-life. Can you imagine James Bond hiding refugees in his flat? Foley did – frequently. When asked why he did all this, his answer was simple: 'Because I am a Christian.'

The whole issue of refugees and 'asylum seekers' is currently controversial. We neglect the fact that refugees bring a great deal to a host nation. Much that is 'normal' in our commercial and popular culture (shopping in Marks and Spencer, going out for a balti or a pizza) owes a great deal to previous waves of refugee immigration. As a child, Jesus himself became an asylum-seeker when his family fled Herod's vicious regime by escaping to Egypt.

One issue left undiscussed in the story is this – that many of the families rescued by Foley ended up in Israel/Palestine, the new 'national home' for the Jews. This in turn displaced Palestinian people from their homes, leading to many of the current problems in the modern state of Israel. The Israel/Palestine conflict is just one legacy of Nazi evil.

The story is a composite of characters and incidents detailed in Michael Smith's *Foley – the Spy who Saved 10 000 Jews* (see Bibliography, page 32).

Teaching Suggestions

RE Activities

1 *Ask:* 'What makes a place safe? Where do you feel safe? Why? (Is it something about being a place where you can flourish as a person?)' *Task:* Write a recipe for a safe place.

2 *Study* passages in the psalms (e.g. Psalm 18:1-3, 16-19, Psalm 23, Psalm 27:1-3, Psalm 31:1-5, Psalm 46:1-11, Psalm 71:1-4), looking for examples of images of safety and protection.

Task: What is God compared to in these psalms? Show this in cartoon form. If you were in trouble, which of these would you want God to be like, for you?

3 *Read* James 2:14-17. *Task:* What is this saying about the connection between a person's beliefs and a person's actions? Compare and contrast this with a re-telling of the parable of the Good Samaritan (Luke 10:25-37). Write about someone you admire, whose beliefs are shown in the way they live out their life.

4 In the Bible, God's plans for the Jewish nation (and others living within their borders) included 'cities of refuge' (Joshua 20:1-9), as safe havens for anyone wanting to escape the consequences of a blood feud. This included having a fair trial, and protection under the law.

Task: Read this passage and list the forms of protection it offers for asylum-seekers. Then research what provision *our own* country currently makes for refugees. The Refugee Council on www.refugeecouncil.org.uk/ could be visited for more information and opinions. (Teachers should always visit a website before their pupils, to check suitability for use – some refugee stories can be harrowing.)

Citizenship/PSHE/ Thinking Skills

1. *Discuss:* 'A nation is judged by how it treats the poor and the weak.'
2. 'As we live, we write our own epitaphs.' This suggests that what people say about us after we're dead is based on what we do when we're alive. *Ask:* 'What would you like your own living epitaph to be?'
3. *Task:* Create a list of questions about the story, and then about issues raised in the story.
4. *Task:* Define and discuss what it means to be a refugee. What do you think are right and wrong attitudes to modern asylum-seekers? Write a letter/speech/article that considers some of the arguments.

Language, Literacy and Drama Work

1. *Task:* Imagine you are a chat-show host, interviewing Frank Foley. Create five questions for Frank that will reveal the most important things about him. What answers do you think he would give? Use this to create a pen-picture of the man that reveals something of his hidden character.
2. A long passage from Adèle Geras' *A Candle in the Dark* was used for part of the 1998 KS2 Reading Comprehension SAT (see Bibliography, page 32). It conveys a superb child's eye view of the Kindertransport, when about three thousand German Jewish children were evacuated to families in Britain. The accompanying interview and letters are also helpful. *Read*, and weep.
3. *Task:* Dramatise the scene outside the Embassy, freeze-framing characters and asking them what's going on. (What do you think Frank might have said to the men in uniform, to make them go away? Remember, he had *a lot* of inside information.) Then write a newspaper report based on eye-witness reports of what happened.
4. *Task:* Imagine you are a refugee newly arrived in this country. What drove you to leave your own homeland to come here? What was the journey like? How were you treated when you arrived here? What is it like, living here? Write a letter to someone at home, telling them about it. (This could be a contemporary account based on current news events, or a historical account based on research.)

Glossary

British Embassy – Building(s) in another country where people working for the British government are based.
Berlin – Capital city of Germany.
Passport – Official papers (often made into a booklet) that show who you are. You usually need to take your passport when you go to another country.
Visa – Papers that give you permission to visit or stay in another country.
Diplomat – Here, senior government official in an embassy in another country.
Hospitality – Caring for a visitor.

To the Rescue

Mission

Samuel Papenekis

To the Rescue, pages 3-11 Omnibus I, pages 37-45*

Possible Learning Objectives

This story and the teaching suggestions below give pupils the opportunity to consider:

- how Christianity can flourish in different cultures throughout the world
- Christian teachings that may have motivated the Indians who undertook the rescue mission
- the importance of worship to Christians
- whether it is right to try to persuade others to change their attitudes or religious beliefs

The photocopiable *Mission* activity/assessment sheet (see page 28) focuses on the bravery of the Indians, their faith and culture, and what might help people to be brave in other situations.

Background to the Story

Yes, this all actually happened. When writing his autobiography many years later, Egerton Young recalled the whole episode with a sense of awe. He was amazed at the sheer enthusiasm with which Native American people embraced the Christian gospel and then re-interpreted it in their own culture. As far as he was concerned, the way the Indians 'lived the gospel' proved its true value and made nonsense of the prejudice that many white settlers had against the original inhabitants of the land. For him, Christianity wasn't something that whites forced on native peoples – it was the best possible thing that one culture could share with another.

There is a cynicism in our culture about the idea of 'mission', because it is seen as harmful to indigenous cultures. However, many Christian missionaries have worked hard to understand local customs and not let their own culture become part of their 'message'. The politically significant act of translating the Bible into the local language has enabled many tribal peoples to become literate, and given them a new confidence in their dealings with the outside world.

Teaching Suggestions

RE Activities

1 *Task:* Which parts of the Bible do you think may have influenced Sam and the others on this occasion? Look up the following (see note overleaf) and give a reason for your answer: Proverbs 3:3, Micah 6:8, Matthew 5:7, Matthew 25:31-46, Luke 6:36, Luke 10:25-37.

(More able pupils could be first given the opportunity to think of a few examples for themselves before being provided with examples.)

2 *Task:* Study the words of some traditional Christian prayers or hymns such as the Lord's Prayer (Matthew 6:9-13), 'The Lord is My Shepherd' (Psalm 23), 'Abide with Me' or 'Guide Me, O Thou Great Redeemer (Bread of Heaven)' (see, for example, *Hymns Ancient and Modern* or *Common Praise*). Which sections do you think would mean the most to a group of people about to embark on a dangerous mission to help others? (More able pupils could do the same, studying the words of a Communion service.)

Write a prayer or hymn that could have been said or sung at the last service before the rescue party left.

3 *Task:* Create a job specification for a missionary. Write letters to modern missionary societies requesting more information about their work. If possible, invite into school someone with experience of missionary work to share their experiences. (Be aware that many overseas Churches now send missionaries to work *in* the United Kingdom!)

Citizenship/PSHE/ Thinking Skills

1 *Discuss:*

(a) Is it right for someone to talk about their religious faith with other people? (Should you keep a good idea to yourself, or should you share it?)

(b) Is it right to try and persuade someone else to change their religion? (Is this different to the first question? Perhaps it depends on whether it's right to tell *anybody* else about *anything* that you think could make their life better.)

(c) What would happen if nobody ever tried to persuade anyone else to do something different? Would the world be a better place?

Debate: Stage a prepared debate using propositions based on the questions above. Ask the audience to vote at the start, according to their own opinions – and then afterwards, according to the strengths of the arguments used.

2 *Discuss* the whole idea of placing an area under medical quarantine to prevent the spread of infection. What problems would that pose for people living in that area? How would it affect your life if a quarantine order was imposed on the area where you live? How much would you depend on outside help, if no travel outside the area was allowed?

Language, Literacy and Drama Work

1 *Task:* Imagine you are a newspaper reporter. How would you report this story for readers of the following newspapers:

(a) The Christian Indian Weekly Press
(b) The Canadian Settlers Daily

Would the accounts for these two audiences differ? Why?/Why not?

2 *Task:* Choose six important words from this story and say why they are important. Brainstorm and research the meaning of the word 'mission' (and its use in the story's title) and the word 'hero'.

3 *Task:* Find some of the Canadian locations on a map, and try to chart the possible river journey.

4 *Task:* Research the lives of modern 'First Nation' peoples in the USA and Canada today. (Many have their own websites. These should be checked by teachers in advance for suitability.)

Glossary

Indian – A Native American/First Nation person. The people living in North America were first called 'Indians' when Christopher Columbus and others were trying to sail West from Europe to reach the East Indies, a group of islands near India. Instead, Columbus found 'America', but called the people he found there 'Indians'. Not surprisingly, some of their descendants don't accept this label any more!
White man – European settler.
Quarantine – When a person or area is isolated from others, to stop a disease spreading.
Gospel – Good news. This word is used by Christians to mean the Christian message – the good news about Jesus – and is the title of four books in the Christian Bible about the life of Jesus.
Wigwam – A large round native American dwelling. (The tent is called a tepee.)

The Darkness

Corrie ten Boom

To the Rescue, pages 13-19 Omnibus I, pages 47-53*

Possible Learning Objectives

This story and the teaching suggestions below give pupils the opportunity to consider:

- responses to suffering, including a Christian response
- light and darkness as symbols of good and evil
- aspects of human rights, including how people with learning difficulties should be treated

The photocopiable *The Darkness* activity/assessment sheet (see page 29) focuses on different responses to suffering.

The teaching suggestions for this story complement the activities suggested for:

- *Hospitality*, the story about Frank Foley; see pages 10-12 .

Background to the Story

The story of Corrie ten Boom raises questions about how a supposedly good God can allow such things as the Nazi domination of Europe to happen. Corrie's response was that God doesn't make mistakes, but God does allow himself to work only in certain (mysterious?) ways. She definitely saw the life, death and resurrection of Jesus as the key to solving these mysteries. She could be seen as a simple lady doing her best to be good in a time when it was very difficult, but that would be patronising. Any victim of the Third Reich who worked hard to rehabilitate ex-Nazis deserves nothing but respect.

Teaching Suggestions

RE Activities

1 *Consider:* Think of a time when something really bad happened to you. How did you feel? (Was it somebody's fault?) There are different types of suffering

– sometimes suffering can be the fault of people, and sometimes it just happens. It can make us feel very angry and bitter. What is your own reaction when bad things happen?

Task: What were Corrie's reactions to her own suffering? List them. Why do you think *she* wasn't angry and bitter?

2 *Task:* Corrie believed that God was looking after her even when she was in prison. 'There must be a good reason for his wanting me to be alone with him now,' she said. Some people would be very angry with God for allowing this to happen to them. Would you be? Imagine you are in her situation. What would you say to God? Turn this into a letter or a poem or a prayer.

3 Light and darkness are common symbols around the world. *Brainstorm* words and phrases that show light and darkness to mean good and bad.

Jesus called himself 'The Light of the World'. *Ask:* 'What do you think he meant? What does light do, that he could liken himself to it? (Give direction / clarity / safety?) How was this shown in Corrie's life?'

4 Christians believe that God is in control of the world, but chooses not to do certain things. *Ask:* 'What things do you think God would refuse to do? Why?'

Citizenship/PSHE/ Thinking Skills

1 *Task:* Study a copy of the Universal Declaration of Human Rights. In what way can you see these rights being denied in this story? Where can you see them being affirmed?

2 Corrie spent a great deal of her life working with children with learning difficulties – the Nazis thought such people were worthless, and many were quietly murdered. *Ask:* 'Do you know someone with serious learning difficulties? How do you think we should treat people who cannot do the same things as the rest of us?'

3 Prisons don't need to have bars. *Ask:* 'Can you think of any attitudes we can have that spoil life and make it more difficult for us and other people?'

Language, Literacy and Drama Work

See also RE activities 2 and 3.

1 *Task:* Create an emotions graph to show Corrie's feelings as the story progresses.

2 *Discuss* the imagery contained in the title. *Ask:* 'What things in this story could be termed as "dark" in the metaphorical sense – and as "light"?'

3 *Task:* Create a 'feelings bridge' to show how someone's feelings might progress from 'darkness' (in the metaphorical sense) to 'light'. Label one end of the bridge 'darkness' and the other end 'light'. Where on the bridge would you be if you felt fearful, friendly, curious, isolated, lonely, excited, nervous, confused, confident, reassured? Near one end or somewhere in the middle? Place these feelings on your bridge.

4 *Task:* Turn the conversation in the prison courtyard into a play script – emphasise the changes in tone that would be heard as each character talks about the things that matter to them.

Glossary

Medal ribbons – Strips of coloured fabric sewn onto military uniforms to show that the wearer has been awarded a medal.
Lieutenant – A military rank.
Ration books – When food (or something else) is scarce, it might be 'rationed', to stop some people from buying too much. Your ration book would need to be shown and marked each time you went to buy something that was rationed.
Food stamps – Special tickets allowing certain people to buy food when it is being rationed.

Hunter
The A Rocha Trust

To the Rescue, pages 21-31 Omnibus I, pages 55-65*

Possible Learning Objectives

This story and the teaching suggestions below give pupils the opportunity to consider:

- different attitudes to animals and the environment
- social issues relating to guns

The photocopiable *Hunter* activity/assessment sheet (see page 29) focuses on pupils' own views on some environmental issues.

Background to the Story

Christians haven't always been enthusiastic preservers of the environment, but there have been some remarkable exceptions: St Francis of Assisi thought the birds so important that he spent several hours preaching to them. (Perhaps he was making a point to his human audience.) In medieval times, animals were occasionally put on trial for their misdeeds and given a lawyer to speak on their behalf, because all God's creatures deserved justice. During the last 500 years, the general Western attitude was that the world and its creatures were 'ours' to use as we saw fit – but today, many people think differently.

The environmentalist movement has led many to change their attitudes to continuing 'development', and a continuing series of ecological disasters has made many Western governments change some policies. However, many 'developing' countries now undergoing industrialisation do not take kindly to Western sermons about good housekeeping. Are *we* prepared to help fund *their* development of cleaner technology? Watch this space...

The A Rocha Trust supports several environmental projects involving young people in both the inner city and the countryside. Do visit their website www.arocha.org to find out more. (Incidentally, the idiot who visited 'Cruzinha' and declared that there were only seven real bird species was yours truly...)

Teaching Suggestions

RE Activities

1 Christians believe that God created the world (although they may not take literally the creation accounts in Genesis 1-2). *Task:* Research one species of bird. Then describe it as if God was describing one of his finest pieces of work. (See also Language, Literacy and Drama task 4.)

2 In the Bible, Philippians 4:8 urges readers to fill their minds with good things. In the story, Emilio stopped thinking about the gun because his mind was full of something more beautiful. *Task:* In pencil, draw a mind full of negative thoughts. What positive things might help to counter these negative and unhelpful thoughts? In ink, write or draw them over the negative thoughts.

3 *Task:* Research the A Rocha Trust and create a data entry for it to go in a leaflet describing the work of different environmental charities. What do the symbols in the A Rocha Trust's logo say about it? Create an alternative logo for the Trust. (What different images could you use that would sum up its work?)

Citizenship/PSHE/ Thinking Skills

1 *Task:* How important is the environment? Role-play a debate. Suppose that developers want to build a holiday resort near a particular beach which is the breeding ground for an endangered species of turtle (e.g. Hawksbill turtle). How would the developers and conservationists argue their cases? Prepare the arguments, then present them – and take a vote on the strength of the arguments. *OR* Debate a local example of a 'developers *vs.* conservationists' issue.

2 *Debate* the reasons for/against taking part in the hunting of wild animals (e.g. foxes, rabbits, deer or hares) for 'sport'.

3 *Discuss* why many children are fascinated by guns. Is this a bad thing in itself? Why do so many children like to imagine they have a gun? Could this be dangerous in future? How much of this is caused by what we see on film and TV and video? (Note how a great deal of media gun-play stems from the USA, where they have very different attitudes to gun control, as illustrated in Michael Moore's 2002 film *Bowling for Columbine*.)

Task: Create a leaflet that tries to persuade shop owners not to sell imitation (toy) handguns to young people. *OR* Compose a letter/e-mail to send to a TV station/film studio expressing concern about excessive screen violence. *OR* Research UK gun laws and set out the main rules on a mini-poster, highlighting especially the health and safety issues.

Language, Literacy and Drama Work

1 *Task:* Collect newspaper reports on the debate about hunting foxes with dogs, researching the arguments used by both sides. Present your findings as a poster.

2 *Task:* Find examples of 'hunting' in children's literature (e.g. Roald Dahl's *Danny, the Champion of the World*). Analyse the plot and characterisation in a passage, to reveal the author's own opinion on the subject.

3 *Task:* Read Psalm 124, which likens escaping from enemies to a bird escaping the hunter's snare. Use 'a bird escaping the hunter' as a metaphor or simile for a situation you might face when you would feel trapped (e.g. being cornered by bullies). Who might be the rescuer? Turn this into a poem, using the 'hunted bird' metaphor.

4 *Task:* Research the migration habits of a range of bird species and prepare a labelled map showing the routes. *OR* Research the habitat and details of one native bird species and create a presentation to show to the rest of the class.

5 *Task:* Produce sorting diagrams to help with the identification of similar-looking bird species.

6 *Task:* Analyse a local wildlife area, mapping out its plant species, animal habitats, and the human impact on the site. Use this information to produce an annotated map. Is it a place *you* could get involved in preserving?

7 *Task:* Investigate other websites with an ecological theme, e.g. those listed below. Make a note of the aims and objectives of each organisation. Discuss their similarities and differences to the A Rocha Trust.

- Red list of threatened species: www.redlist.org
- Royal Society for the Protection of Birds: www.rspb.org
- Wildfowl and Wetlands Trust: www.wwt.org.uk
- Eden Project: www.edenproject.com
- Natural History Museum: www.nhm.ac.uk
- World Conservation Monitoring Centre: www.unep-wcmc.org
- Naturenet: www.naturenet.net

All websites should be checked for suitability before use by pupils.

Glossary

Telescopic sights – A device on a gun to help you see the target close up.
Species – A group of living things that can breed with each other.
Predator – A creature that hunts other creatures for food.

It's Tough at the Top

Riot!

Toyohiko Kagawa

It's Tough at the Top, pages 3-13 Omnibus I, pages 67-77*

Possible Learning Objectives

This story and the teaching suggestions below give pupils the opportunity to consider:

- what is involved in being a peacemaker
- how religious faith or personal beliefs can influence important decisions people make about their lifestyle and actions
- whether or not protests against injustice should be non-violent
- what makes a good leader
- protection of workers' rights

The photocopiable *Riot!* activity/assessment sheet (see page 30) focuses on Kagawa's Christian beliefs and important features of his life and work.

The teaching suggestions for this story complement the activities suggested for:

- *Surrender*, the story about Chris Keeble; see pages 22-24;
- *Peacemaker*, the story about Pocohontas; see pages 24-26.

Background to the Story

Europeans who visit modern Japan find an amazing collision of Western and Japanese cultures, both traditional and modern. The Christian Church there has been criticised for being heavily 'Westernised' and 'foreign'. However, Toyohiko Kagawa is an example of a man who was thoroughly Japanese and thoroughly Christian; his faith had a depth that made 'cultural' issues irrelevant because it was amazingly simple and deep. He loved God and loved his neighbour with an intensity that overwhelmed cynics – and his hard-headed appraisal of social issues won him immense respect.

Teaching Suggestions

RE Activities

1 *Discuss* the main points of the story, drawing out the idea that Kagawa had already won a reputation for being a friend of the poor at the point where this story starts. Map out the biographical details of his early life, showing how decisions made then would lead on to bigger things later.

2 *Task:* Study the Bible passages Matthew 5:1-10, Matthew 5:38-39, Matthew 6:19-21, Matthew 6:24. What do you think Kagawa would have said they mean? How did he live them out in his own life? What might have been the consequences if he had chosen to live his life differently?

3 *Ask:* 'What do *you* believe in? Do you have any big ideas that motivate you? What are they? (Can you sum them up in a few words?) How do you think they will affect your future when you have to make important decisions?'

Citizenship/PSHE/ Thinking Skills

1 Should protests against injustice be non-violent? *Discuss* 'direct action' and the consequences of making violent protests (e.g. about a hot topic like animal rights). What can peaceful protests achieve? (Pupils could research the ideas of Gandhi and Martin Luther King for more ideas on this topic.)

2 *Task:* What makes a good leader? Discuss and list the qualities of leadership – and then write the recipe for it!

3 *Task:* Research trade unions, and their role in the protection of workers' rights. Find out the rules for joining or forming a trade union at a place of work. Invite a trade union representative in, to explain how they work. (Many unions have their own websites. Check before use.)

Language, Literacy and Drama Work

1 *Task:* Imagine you are the editor for this Superstars series of books about people who made a difference to the world. Sum up the arguments for including this story.

2 *Task:* Create an emotions line graph detailing the highs and lows of how Kagawa felt as the story progressed. *OR* Create an imaginary map showing the same thing.

3 *Task:* Different people of the time would have thought rather differently about Kagawa! There would have been a lot of information about him written down in police files. What would they have said about him? (Would it all be accurate?)

(a) Write Kagawa's police file in note form.
(b) Imagine you are a news reporter. Write the story of the dockers' protest for your newspaper. How will you report the role of Kagawa?
(c) Now compose a mini-biography (exactly 50 words) that gives the main points about the life of Toyohiko Kagawa.

4 *Task:* Devise a front cover for a video of Kagawa's life and write the back-cover blurb. What would the video's title be?

5 *Task:* In groups, re-enact the scene outside the town hall, designing and making the protest banners to be used. Make sure every character has worked out *who* they are and *why* they are there.

6 *Task:* Create a haiku about one aspect of the story. (A haiku is a Japanese-style three-line poem with 17 syllables in the pattern 5-7-5.) Make the first line a summary of the issue, the second line a description, and the third a comment.

Glossary

Trade union – An organised association of workers in a trade (particular type of job), formed to protect their rights and interests.
Slums – Very poor areas in a city.
Pacifist – Someone who does not believe that any war is worth fighting.

Surrender

Chris Keeble

It's Tough at the Top, pages 15-21 Omnibus I, pages 79-85*

Possible Learning Objectives

This story and the teaching suggestions below give pupils the opportunity to consider:

- difficulties leaders may face, such as having to make tough decisions
- prayer as a response to difficult situations
- negotiation as a way of resolving disputes

The photocopiable *Surrender* activity/assessment sheet (see page 31) focuses on prayer.

The teaching suggestions for this story complement the activities suggested for:

- *Riot!*, the story about Toyohiko Kagawa; see pages 20-21;
- *Peacemaker*, the story about Pocohontas; see pages 24-26.

Background to the Story

The Falklands War of 1982-3 was memorable for many things – but the Argentinian defeat (and the death of 750 of its servicemen) brought down a brutal military regime that had wiped out 20 000 dissidents since 1976. Was the British victory actually a Good Thing for Argentina? Perhaps it is still too early to tell.

Teaching Suggestions

RE Activities

1 *Discuss* what prayer is, aiming for a class definition, and comparing this with some dictionary definitions. *Ask:* 'Are there different types of prayer?' (Christian prayers are often classified using the acronym ACTS: Adoration, Confession, Thanks and Supplication, i.e. making requests.) *Explain* that there are many different ideas about this, but also that many people find prayer a real help in their lives. *List together* a range of situations where people might want to pray.

2 *Together, study* some famous Christian prayers. (See *Surrender* activity/assessment sheet, page 31, for examples.) *Ask:* 'In what ways are they similar – and different? Which one might be helpful for someone having a difficult time? Do you have a particular favourite?'

3 *Ask:* 'Can you suggest ways in which it might be helpful to pray for your enemy?'

4 *Task:* Create a display of famous prayers and personal prayers, with objects used to help prayer (beads, symbols, pictures, …). *Discuss:* 'What items would *you* carry with you, to provide comfort in a crisis?'

5 *Task:* Write a private prayer of your own that expresses to God your thoughts about a situation that's important to you. [It is important to make clear to pupils the intended audience for such a prayer. Will it be something that may be read out in class, or put on display for others to read?] *OR* Write a prayer that a Christian (or someone else) could use for a given situation.

6 *Show* examples of the symbols of peace: the dove, the olive branch, the rainbow. *Explain* that these are based on the biblical story of Noah (Genesis 6-9). *Ask:* 'In what ways did Chris Keeble make peace with his enemies?'

Citizenship/PSHE/ Thinking Skills

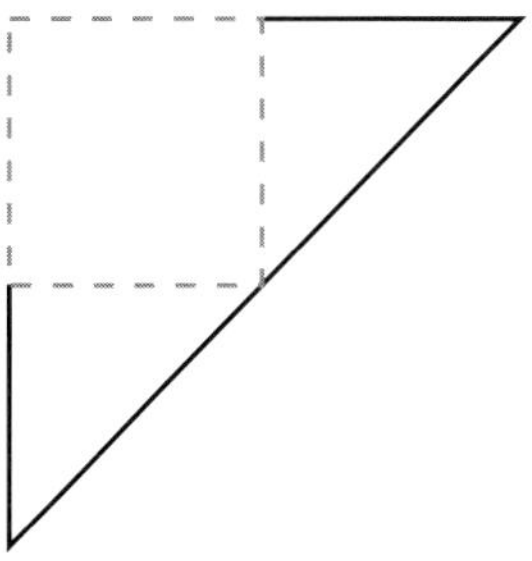

1 In a difficult situation, it can be hard to make a choice – but sometimes, there may be choices available that we haven't thought about. *Set* a 'lateral thinking' puzzle as an illustration of this. (*Example:* Draw a square. Set the task of drawing a triangle on the square that touches all four corners. It can't be done, of course – unless you realise that the triangle can have sides extending further than the square itself.)

2 *Ask:* 'Can you think of real-life situations (in the news?) where there may be choices available (and possible solutions) that haven't been considered yet?'

3 *Discuss* the quality and value of negotiation as a way of resolving disputes – Chris Keeble later said that it helps to sort things out if you can think your way into your enemy's problems. *Ask:* 'Can you think of situations where it would help if you could see the other person's point of view?'

4 *Together, list* the names or roles of leaders that you know. *Discuss and list* the attributes that make a good leader. *Ask:* 'When do you think it is hard to be a leader?'

Task: Leadership can be seen as a kind of burden that you have to carry. Create an envelope that looks like a rucksack. On slips of paper, write the burdens you think have to be carried by a leader, and place them inside. Which burden would be the heaviest?

Language, Literacy and Drama Work

1 *Task:* Re-enact key events in the story, freeze-framing the events of that night. Then 'hot seat' the two captured prisoners, before, during, and after their meeting with Chris Keeble. Do this with some British soldiers from 2 Para as well. Discuss their thoughts and feelings before, during, and after – what do they think could happen next? Classify these thoughts as Positive, Negative – and Interesting (PIN – an acronym used by Edward de Bono; see Bibliography, page 32)!

2 *Task:* Study the soliloquy by Shakespeare's Henry V on the night before the battle of Agincourt. Compare this with Mark 14:32-42, which includes Jesus' prayer in the Garden of Gethsemane. What do they both say about the difficulties of leadership? (For classroom purposes, using the videos of Kenneth Branagh's *Henry the Fifth* and the animated life of Jesus *The Miracle Maker* would complement this.)

3 *Task:* What do you think the soldiers on the opposing sides in the story would have wanted? Use your answers to create a peace declaration that clearly explains what will happen if the Argentinian soldiers agree to lay down their arms.

4 *Task:* Create a class poem about peace where everybody writes one line.

Glossary

Paratroopers – Special soldiers trained to land from the air by parachute or helicopter.
Battalion – Group of (about) 1000 soldiers.

Regiment – Larger group of soldiers (usually several battalions), commanded by a colonel.
Airfield – Base where combat aircraft can take off and land.
Camouflage netting – Multi-coloured covering that makes it difficult for the enemy to see you.
Mortars – Small rockets that shoot up, then come down like bombs on the enemy.
Ammunition – Bullets and other things to fire at the enemy.
National anthem – A special song associated with a particular country.
Truce – An agreement to stop fighting.
Reinforcements – Extra soldiers who come and help.
Full military honours – Special ways of showing respect at funerals for members of the armed forces
Democratic government – Government chosen by everybody voting in a fair election.

Peacemaker

Pocohontas

It's Tough at the Top, pages 23-31 Omnibus I, pages 87-95*

Possible Learning Objectives

This story and the teaching suggestions below give pupils the opportunity to consider:

- different styles of leadership
- what Jesus said about being a leader
- what it means to be a Christian
- skills required to be a peacemaker

The story also refers to the Authorised (King James) Version of the Bible in English, the early history of smoking, and the tobacco trade.

The photocopiable *Peacemaker* activity/assessment sheet (see page 30) focuses on possible approaches to peacemaking in school situations.

The teaching suggestions for this story complement the activities suggested for:

- *Riot!*, the story about Toyohiko Kagawa; see pages 20-21;
- *Surrender*, the story about Chris Keeble; see pages 22-24.

Background to the Story

History is not always recorded by the people who make it. The story of Pocohontas was told by the British people who settled in her homeland, and not by the original inhabitants. Her profession of Christian faith is on record, but we have little information about her own thoughts and feelings as two cultures collided head-on. She certainly did visit London and the royal court, but there is little obvious evidence for her actually meeting King James in the way described here. (That doesn't mean it didn't happen, of course.) She never went home, but died of the tuberculosis that claimed so many Indians who came to Britain, probably through a lack of inherited immunity.

Teaching Suggestions

RE Activities

1 *Task:* In the story, Pocohontas reflects on the different qualities she sees in her father Powhatan and in King James. List these qualities, and then study the following Bible passages to find out how Jesus saw his own leadership: Luke 22:24-27, John 13:1-17, John 18:33-37.

How do you think Jesus would have viewed Powhatan or King James? Create some cardboard crowns illustrated with the different rights and responsibilities that a king (or any leader) should have, according to Jesus.

2 *Task:* What do you think a Christian is? Write down your definition, then find out some more definitions and compare them with yours. (Pupils could consult textbooks, etc., or ask Christians and others for their definitions. They should use at least one reference source from the Christian Church.) Are you surprised at the variations? Why? Why not? Now write a job specification for a Christian, listing essential/desirable qualities.

3 *Ask:* 'What is a peacemaker?' *Suggest* a playground dispute between two people (a penalty decision in football?) that needs arbitration by a third party. *Brainstorm* the skills and qualities someone would need to defuse, then resolve the conflict.

Read what the Bible says in Galatians 5:22-23 about the qualities that God wants to give people. *Ask:* 'Which of these do you think are the ones a peacemaker needs most?' *Discuss* how important peacemaking is nowadays. *Read and discuss* what the Bible says about its importance in Proverbs 12:20, Matthew 5:9, James 3:18. ('Righteousness' could be translated as 'fairness that is pleasing to God'.)

Citizenship/PSHE/ Thinking Skills

1 *Ask:* 'What makes a place peaceful?' Collect definitions. *Ask:* 'Would you want to live there? Why? Why not?' Many definitions of peace tend to be negative – describing places where nothing interesting is happening! *Explain* that for many people, peace has a wider, positive definition, involving justice. *Ask:* 'If peace is about things being fair, what would make our world more peaceful?'

Task: Write about 'My Ideas for a Peaceful World'.

2 *Distribute and discuss* suitable newspaper articles involving unfairness. *Together, list* (a) examples of situations where people are suffering because of genuine unfairness and (b) positive examples where genuine efforts have been made to make things fairer. *Sort and display* the articles under the headings 'Peace?' and 'No Peace?'

3 *Suggest* to pupils a modern situation that needs some peacemaking. (This could be a national issue or something much closer to home.) *Task:* Research the different viewpoints, and then stage an arbitration-type meeting about the subject 'in character'.

Language, Literacy and Drama Work

1 *Task:* Write a letter home from Pocohontas to her father, contrasting the lives of the English with those of her own people.

2 *Task:* People in this story sometimes say one thing and think something different. Find some examples, copy out the dialogue in speech bubbles then add the speakers' hidden thoughts in thought bubbles.

3 *Task:* Draw a human outline. Inside it, write words that describe the character of Pocohontas. Around the outside, describe things that happened to her and influenced her.

4 *Task:* View some of the websites suggested in the information panel 'What really happened', then write a version of the Pocohontas story that you think is as accurate as possible. Give reasons why this is most likely to be accurate.

5 *Task:* Research historical details referred to in the story, e.g. life at the royal court of the Tudors or Stuarts, the history of tobacco and smoking, the Gunpowder Plot, the translation of the Authorised Version of the Bible, places named after monarchs or other famous people (Why do you think they were given that name?), Indian tribes and European settlement in North America.

6 *Task:* Create a time-line for events given in the story or information boxes, for the period surrounding the lifetimes of Pocohontas and King James the First.

7 *Task:* View a section of the Disney film, and re-write a short portion so it becomes historically accurate. Analyse some song lyrics from the film to discover what they reveal about modern attitudes to the story. Write a letter of praise and/or complaint to the Disney organisation about their treatment of historical material.

8 *Task:* Create a collage of adverts for cigarettes, and then create anti-smoking posters using similar imagery!

Glossary

Court – Place where the King met his subjects in public and met advisors and ambassadors.
Pike – Spear with an axe head near the end.
Hostage – Somebody taken prisoner to force somebody *else* to do something.
Colony – Settlement within a country that is ruled by the government of another country.
Eden – Perfect place, like the Garden of Eden in the Book of Genesis in the Bible.
Tribal elders – Men of experience who helped a chief to make decisions.
Authorised – Commanded to happen or approved by someone in authority.
Hybrid – Of mixed origin.
Tuberculosis – Disease of the lungs that people can catch in damp conditions.

Better and Better!

1. In the table, list five of the subjects you are being taught in school. For each one, give yourself a mark out of 10 that shows how well you think you are doing in that subject. Then explain what it is you find easy or hard about it. Don't just say that you are good or bad at this subject, or that you like it! Try to think **why.**

Subject	Mark	Reasons

2. What is your 'best' subject? What skills do you have that make it your best subject?

   My best subject is .... I can ....

3. What other skills do you think you need to keep improving in this subject?

   I now need to learn how to ....

4. What steps do you need to take to help you to learn or develop those skills?

   I could start by ....

Wings

War **Danger**

Death **Friends**

Work **Family**

1. What do we know about Cyril from the story? List any facts near the picture.
2. What do we know about his attitudes to what he was doing? List any facts near the words.
3. In your opinion, how did those attitudes affect the way he died?

   ....

4. The Victoria Cross is awarded to men and women in the armed forces who have shown immense bravery. What kind of bravery do you admire? Design a medal to award to someone showing that kind of bravery. Who would you give it to? Why?

Safe and Sound

1. What things does a small child need to feel safe? Draw and label them, around the picture of this child.

2. What sorts of things would someone your own age need, to feel safe?

3. Imagine you are a refugee arriving in this country with only the clothes you're wearing. What things would you need, to help you to feel safe?

4. What did Frank Foley do to help people to feel safe?

5. Imagine a pupil is joining your class for the first time. What things do you think you should do to make that person feel welcome – and safe? Write about this. Do you think welcoming a new pupil is important? Say why or why not.

Dangerous Mission

1. Imagine that Sam or one of the other Indians in the boats looked into the river at the beginning of the journey and saw not only their face reflected back, but also their thoughts and feelings. What would they have seen? Write these thoughts and feelings in the water.

2. Suppose that Sam and the others were given a medal when they returned. What would the citation have said? (A citation says why someone has been given a medal or an award.)

   Design the medal and write the citation. The design should reflect Sam's culture as well as his Christian faith.

3. We don't have to face the situation Sam faced, but we often have to be brave. Think about ordinary situations where people have to be brave. How might religious faith help in those situations? What else might help? Write your answer or present it as a series of pictures with notes.

Suffering

1 What do you think 'suffering' means? Write your own dictionary definition here, then discuss it with a partner.

suffering

....

....

2 Study these statements about suffering. Do you agree or disagree with them? On each axis (line), mark a cross to show how much you agree or disagree with each statement. For example, if you agree strongly put your cross at the left-hand end.

Suffering is always bad.
Agree ———————————— Disagree

If you are suffering, it must be your own fault.
Agree ———————————— Disagree

Suffering can sometimes teach us important lessons for life.
Agree ———————————— Disagree

Suffering can be a good thing.
Agree ———————————— Disagree

Suffering happens to everybody.
Agree ———————————— Disagree

3 Now share your answers with somebody else. Do they agree with you?

4 Write a summary of your own thoughts about suffering. Consider the following questions as you plan your answer:

- What are the different types of suffering that people can go through?
- In what ways do different people try to cope with suffering or explain it?
- Do you think suffering is always bad – or good? Why?
- Think of a time when either you were suffering, or someone you know was suffering. What helped you or them to get through it?
- Finally, what would be the best advice or help you could offer someone else who was suffering?

How Important Are Animals?

1 How important are animals? When should human beings come first? Use these statements to work out your own ideas about environmental issues. Put a cross along the axis (line) to show your opinion.

Human beings are the most important creatures on this planet.
Agree ———————————— Disagree

Animals are worth as much as people.
Agree ———————————— Disagree

We should care about the environment only when we can afford to.
Agree ———————————— Disagree

It is wrong to use animals for food.
Agree ———————————— Disagree

It is wrong to keep animals as pets.
Agree ———————————— Disagree

Farmers have the right to kill wild animals that are damaging their crops or livestock.
Agree ———————————— Disagree

We should always preserve areas with ecosystems (special local environments) that sustain rare plants or animals.
Agree ———————————— Disagree

Human beings damage the planet, and there should be fewer of them.
Agree ———————————— Disagree

2 Compare your answers with a partner. Are there areas you broadly agree/disagree on? List your agree/disagree issues.

3 What would happen if lots of people agreed with you on each issue? What changes might happen? Would this make things better, or would it generate more problems? Suppose every government agreed with your ideas, and did everything that you suggested to help preserve the environment. How would the world be different in 10 years' time? Write about it.

A Christian in Action

1 In the story, Kagawa shows his Christian beliefs in what he does and says. What key Christian beliefs held by Kagawa can you see in action in the story? Write about them on the jigsaw pieces. Possible headings could be 'Justice and fairness', 'Violence', 'God', 'What people are worth'.

2 Choose four important things about the life and work of Toyohiko Kagawa. List or draw them in this diamond in ranking order, with the most important (no. 1) at the top. (How do you think *he* would have placed them?)

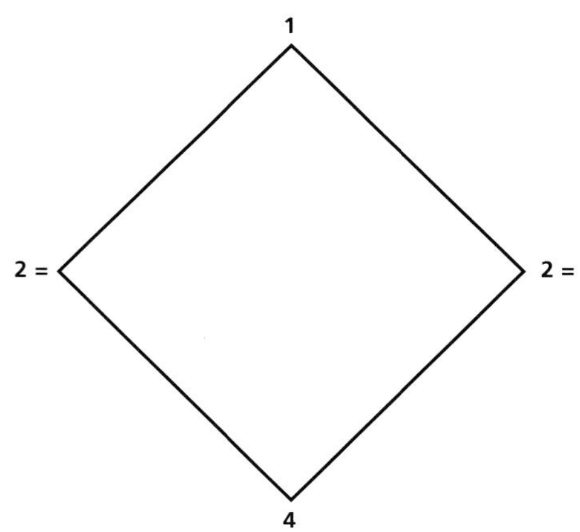

Could You Be a Peacemaker?

Could you be a peacemaker? It's harder than it looks! Some schools appoint older pupils as 'playground buddies', who are volunteers with the job of sorting out playground arguments before they get nasty. Study the real-life situations in the boxes, and work out your strategy for solving one or more of these problems. (Some problems, of course, may have to be sorted out by a responsible adult!) You may need more information before you reach your solution. Note down things you need to find out and your suggestions for solving the problem on another piece of paper, like this.

Problem:	
Extra things I need to find out	**My suggestions to help sort out the problem**

A A game of football has been organised in the playground. Tom, the owner of the ball, has said he doesn't want Paul to play, because he 'doesn't like' him. Paul is angry, because he usually plays football with the others – but today, Tom is the only one with a ball. A fight is about to break out between the two of them.

B Sarah is furious with Katie, because Katie is now a close friend with Ravinder. Sarah has always been 'best friends' with Katie, but Ravinder has just joined the class from another school. There has been some nasty name-calling during morning break, and everyone is feeling hurt.

C There is an argument about collector cards. Ciaran has brought his collection from home to show his friends, but some now seem to be missing, and he is saying that somebody stole them from his bag. He thinks Sam (one of his friends) has got them.

D Apesh complains that everyone in his class is picking on him. They all deny it, saying he's just making a fuss about nothing.

E During a playground argument over a game, Taranjit has started verbally abusing Scott, saying things about his mother. Scott replied by saying something about Taranjit's sister. They are both threatening to tell their older brothers.

What is Prayer?

What is prayer? There are lots of answers to this question. The statements in the speech bubbles are some examples. Do you agree or disagree with these statements? Grade these comments on a 1-5 basis, where 1 means 'I don't agree at all', 5 means 'I completely agree'. Below each grading, give a reason for your answer.

"Praying is about making a shopping list and giving it to God."

Grading: ....

Reason: ....

"Prayer is about trying to listen hard to what God is saying – so you can obey God better."

Grading: ....

Reason: ....

"Prayer is the most natural thing in the world – when you think hard and try to make sense of it all, then you are praying."

Grading: ....

Reason: ....

"Prayer is like a drowning man asking for a lifebelt."

Grading: ....

Reason: ....

"Prayer is just arguing with the weather."

Grading: ....

Reason: ....

2 Some prayers are very popular, and have often been turned into posters or small cards to carry in a wallet or purse. Many are learned by heart. Read the Christian prayers on this page. Pick one, copy it out and illustrate it, showing a situation where somebody might want to be able to use a prayer like this.

My Father,
I abandon myself to your will.
Do with me as you will.
Whatever you may do with
me, I thank you.
Provided your will is fulfilled
I ask for nothing more.

Our Father in heaven,
Hallowed be your name.
Your kingdom come,
Your will be done,
On earth as it is in heaven.
Give us each day our daily
bread,
And forgive us our sins,
As we forgive those who sin
against us,
And lead us not into
temptation,
But deliver us from the evil
one.

Lord,
Give me courage to face the
things in my life that can be
changed,
Peace of mind about those
things that can't,
And wisdom, so I can tell the
difference between them.

Lord,
Tomorrow I will be very busy.
I may forget you.
Please don't *you* forget me.

Bibliography

For More Background to the Stories

The Man Who Was 'Q' – The Life of Charles Fraser-Smith David Porter (Paternoster Press, 1989)

The Secret War of Charles Fraser-Smith Charles Fraser-Smith *et al.* (Michael Joseph, 1981)

Cyril Joe Barton V.C. WW Lowther (Wear Books, 1994)

Foley: The Spy who Saved 10 000 Jews Michael Smith (Coronet, 1999)

By Canoe and Dog-Train Egerton Young (Out of print but worth looking out for in libraries or second-hand bookshops)

Corrie – Watchmaker's Daughter Jean Watson (Kingsway, 1982)

Saint in the Slums Cyril Davey (Lutterworth, 1968). About Toyohiko Kagawa.

Japanese Religion Japanese Agency for Cultural Affairs (Kodansha International Ltd, 1972)

Resources for Teaching Suggestions

Children Solving Problems Edward de Bono (Penguin, 1972)

Use Your Head Tony Buzan (BBC Consumer Publishing, 2000)

The Anti-Colouring Book Susan Striker (Hippo Books, 1986)

George Herbert's poem 'Easter-wings' and can be found in *The Complete English Poems* (George Herbert, Viking Penguin, 1992) or viewed on the internet at www.pjbsware.demon.co.uk

A Candle in the Dark Adèle Geras (A & C Black, 1995). For activities relating to this, a useful website to visit is www.storiesfromtheweb.org

Recommended for any research into Christian mission: Partnership House Mission Studies Library, 157 Waterloo Road, London SE1 8XA.
Tel: 020 7928 8681. Direct dial: 020 7803 3215. Fax: 020 7928 3627.
E-mail: library.phmslib@cms-uk.org

This book has been published in association with The Stapleford Centre.

The Stapleford Centre is an interdenominational charity which produces materials and offers in-service courses to resource the teaching of Christianity in schools. Full details of courses and publications are available from:

The Stapleford Centre,
The Old Lace Mill,
Frederick Road,
Stapleford,
Nottingham, NG9 8FN
Tel: 0115 939 6270
Fax: 0115 939 2076
E-mail: **admin@stapleford-centre.org**
Website: **www.stapleford-centre.org**

THE STAPLEFORD CENTRE

Religious and Moral Education Press
A division of SCM-Canterbury Press Ltd
A wholly owned subsidiary of Hymns Ancient & Modern Ltd
St Mary's Works, St Mary's Plain, Norwich, Norfolk NR3 3BH

First published 2004

ISBN 1 85175 312 5

Designed and typeset by TOPICS – The Creative Partnership, Exeter

Illustrations by David Johnson

Printed in Great Britain by Halstan and Co. Ltd, Amersham, Buckinghamshire for SCM-Canterbury Press Ltd, Norwich

Acknowledgements
Grateful thanks are due to the following:

Margaret Cooling, Tracy Holmes and Gordon Raggett, both for their ideas and suggestions for teacher activities, and also for general encouragement.

Alison Farnell and Wylva Davis of the Stapleford Centre for seeing through the contractual negotiations and school trialling.

Chris Keeble, Marcial Felgueiras (A Rocha Trust) and Joyce Vosey (Cyril Barton's sister), for their personal advice and support.

The staff and children of the following schools for their help with trialling stories and lesson material, and for giving valuable feedback:

St Matthew's Bloxam, CE Primary School, Rugby
Rosslyn Junior School, Aspley, Nottingham
Coughton CE VC Primary, Warks
St John's CE Primary School, Stapleford, Nottingham
St Anne's CE Primary School, Wigan
Elm Wood Primary School, Manchester
Scargill CE Primary School, West Hallam, Ilkeston, Derbyshire
All Saints CE (A) Primary School, Wigston, Leicester
Richard Hill Primary School, Thurcaston, Leicester
Parkview Primary School, Oakwood, Derby
Bishops' High C of E, Chester
Calder, High School, Halifax
Hadden Park High School, Bilborough, Nottingham
Loughborough Grammar School, Loughborough, Leics
Outwood Grange School, Wakefield
Greysbrooke Primary School, Shenstone, Lichfield

Lin Jennings of St Matthew's Bloxam School, for extra help and feedback after trialling.

And finally, to my wife Rachel, for enduring all those happy hours I've spent researching and tapping away at a keyboard – thank you for all your encouragement and endurance. I married a wise woman!